cleared for takeoff

Charting Your Career in the Pilot's Seat

roger smith

Copyright © 2024 by Roger Smith

All rights reserved.

No part of this book may be reproduced in any form or by any electronic or mechanical means, including information storage and retrieval systems, without written permission from the author, except for the use of brief quotations in a book review.

contents

1. THE DREAM OF FLIGHT ... 7
   The Gateway to the Skies ... 7
   Trailblazers of the Sky ... 10
   The Role of an Airline Pilot Today ... 12

2. EDUCATIONAL PATHWAYS ... 17
   Blueprints to the Pilot's Seat ... 17
   Navigating the Flight Path: A Guide to Aviation Education ... 20
   The Academic and Certification Ladder in Aviation ... 23

3. GETTING YOUR WINGS ... 27
   Earning Your Wings: The Journey to a Private Pilot License ... 27
   Ascending to New Heights: The Commercial Pilot License ... 30
   The Captain's Journey: Mastering the Airline Transport Pilot License ... 32

4. BUILDING EXPERIENCE ... 37
   Chronicles of the Sky: The Pilot's Logbook ... 37
   Mentorship in the Skies: The Role of Flight Instructors ... 40
   Taking Flight: Regional Airlines as Career Launchpads ... 42

5. THE HIRING PROCESS — 47
Clearing the Runway: Understanding Airline Application Requirements — 47
The Final Approach: Mastering the Airline Interview and Selection Process — 51
The Art of Simulation: A Pilot's Guide to Simulator Assessments — 55

6. LIFE IN THE COCKPIT — 59
The Dynamics of Airline Operations: A Comprehensive Overview — 59
Navigating the Skies: The Pilot's Role in Modern Aviation — 63
Sunrise to Sunset: The Pilot's Journey — 66

7. ADVANCED TRAINING AND CERTIFICATIONS — 71
Mastering the Machines: The Journey Through Type Ratings — 71
Elevating Expertise: The Cycle of Recurrent Training and Checks — 74
Commanding the Skies: The Ascent to Captaincy — 78

8. NAVIGATING A PILOT'S CAREER — 83
Charting the Course: Pilots' Pathways in Aviation — 83
Navigating the Hierarchy: The Influence of Seniority in Aviation — 87
Broadening Horizons: Embracing the World Stage of Aviation — 90

9. CHALLENGES AND REWARDS — 95
Harmonizing Altitudes: The Pilot's Quest for Work-Life Balance — 95
The Thrill of Flying — 98
Financial and Personal Rewards — 101

10. THE FUTURE OF AVIATION 105
Technological Advancements: Elevating
Aviation Conversations 105
The Role of Pilots in Future Aviation 108
Preparing for Changes in the Industry 110

Epilogue: Beyond the Horizon 115

1 / the dream of flight

the gateway to the skies

EMBARKING on the journey to become an airline pilot is akin to learning a new language, one that allows you to converse with the skies. The allure of aviation is not just in the mechanics of aircraft or the physics of flight, but also in the intricate dance of communication that occurs between pilots, air traffic controllers, and the aircraft itself. It's a symphony of technical jargon, quick decision-making, and clear directives that ensure the safety and efficiency of air travel.

To truly understand aviation, one must first appreciate the rich tapestry of its history. It's a narrative filled with daring dreams, groundbreaking innovations, and relentless pursuit of pushing boundaries. The Wright brothers' first powered flight in 1903 was not merely a leap in transportation; it was the ignition of a global transformation. Since then, the field of aviation has soared to incredible heights, with airline pilots becoming the modern-day navigators of this expansive domain.

As we delve deeper into the essence of aviation, it becomes clear that it is much more than operating an aircraft. It's about understanding the language of the skies – the weather patterns, the air currents, and the invisible pathways that crisscross the atmosphere. Pilots are trained to read these signs, to interpret the subtle cues that nature provides, and to respond with precision and grace.

The path to becoming an airline pilot is rigorous and demanding, requiring a blend of academic knowledge and practical skills. It begins with a foundational understanding of aerodynamics, where one learns about lift, thrust, drag, and weight – the four forces that dictate an aircraft's movement. This knowledge is crucial, as it forms the basis of all flight operations and decisions.

From there, the journey continues with mastering the principles of navigation. In the early days of flight, pilots relied on visual cues and simple maps to find their way. Today, the art of navigation has evolved into a complex system that utilizes advanced technology such as GPS, radar, and various flight management systems. Yet, the core skill remains the same – the ability to chart a course and follow it with unwavering focus.

Communication is the heartbeat of aviation. It's the thread that connects all aspects of a flight, from pre-flight briefings to in-flight adjustments and post-flight debriefs. Pilots must be adept at conveying information clearly and concisely, whether it's reporting their position to air traffic control or discussing technical issues with the crew. This skill is honed through countless hours of practice, where every word spoken is intentional and every instruction is precise.

Safety is the paramount concern in aviation, and it is embedded in every aspect of a pilot's training and responsibilities. It's a mindset that prioritizes caution, preparedness, and constant vigilance. Pilots are trained to anticipate potential issues and to have contingency plans for every conceivable scenario. This proactive approach to safety is what makes air travel one of the safest modes of transportation.

The life of an airline pilot is one of discipline, dedication, and continuous learning. It's a profession that demands the highest standards of professionalism and personal conduct. Pilots are not just operators of complex machinery; they are leaders, decision-makers, and ambassadors of the aviation community.

As we explore the intricacies of aviation, we uncover a world that is both challenging and rewarding. It's a career that offers the opportunity to connect continents, to bridge cultures, and to touch the lives of thousands of passengers. The journey is long, and the responsibilities are great, but for those who hear the call of the skies, there is no greater honor than to answer it.

trailblazers of the sky

The narrative of airline pilots is not merely a chronicle of individuals steering aircraft across the heavens; it is a saga of courage, innovation, and the relentless pursuit of mastery over the skies. The history of these aviators is as much about the human spirit as it is about the evolution of technology and the expansion of our world.

In the nascent days of aviation, pilots were intrepid souls who took to the air in machines that were as much a testament to their bravery as to their ingenuity. These early aviators were not just pilots; they were pioneers, engineers, and dreamers rolled into one. They pushed the boundaries of what was possible, charting courses over lands and seas that had never before been crossed by air.

As the 20th century progressed, the role of the airline pilot began to take shape. The advent of World War I saw pilots taking to the skies in combat, but it also accelerated advancements in aircraft technology and navigation. Post-war, these developments paved the way for commercial aviation, with pilots transitioning from military service to civilian roles, carrying mail and eventually passengers.

The 1920s and '30s saw the golden age of aviation, where pilots like Charles Lindbergh and Amelia Earhart captured the public's imagination. They were not just flying; they were crafting narratives of adventure and exploration. Their feats were not solely personal triumphs but were symbolic of the progress of aviation and the potential it held.

The role of the airline pilot was further solidified with the establishment of scheduled air services. Pilots became the custodians of a new era of travel, shrinking the world map and connecting distant lands. They were no longer lone adventurers but part of a larger system that required precision, discipline, and a deep understanding of the science of flight.

The mid-20th century brought about the jet age, revolutionizing air travel with speed and efficiency previously unimaginable. Airline pilots were at the forefront of this transformation, adapting to new technologies and regulations. They became specialists, mastering complex systems and procedures to ensure the safety and comfort of their passengers.

As we moved into the latter part of the century and beyond, the airline pilot's role continued to evolve. The introduction of automation and advanced avionics changed the nature of piloting, requiring a new set of skills. Pilots had to become adept at managing sophisticated computer systems, all while maintaining the fundamental principles of airmanship.

Today, airline pilots stand as the epitome of professionalism in a field that is ever-changing. They are the synthesis of the past and the present – drawing from the legacy of the trailblazers who came before them and embracing the advancements that define modern aviation. They navigate not just the physical skies but also the complex regulatory and operational environments that govern global air travel.

The history of airline pilots is a testament to human progress. From open cockpits and leather helmets to pressurized cabins and state-of-the-art head-up displays, pilots have been the constant thread, adapting and leading the way. They are the embodiment of our desire to explore, to connect, and to soar beyond our earthly bounds.

the role of an airline pilot today

In the contemporary tapestry of aviation, the airline pilot emerges not merely as a navigator of the skies but as a multifaceted professional, embodying the roles of a safety officer, a technical expert, and a leader. The cockpit they command is a hub of advanced technology and human expertise, where every decision is critical, and every action is a thread in the larger fabric of global connectivity.

The role of an airline pilot today is a complex blend of responsibilities that extend far beyond the act of flying. They are the guardians of a delicate balance between human judgment and technological precision. In the high-altitude office with a view that spans continents, pilots manage sophisticated aircraft systems, ensuring that the symphony of buttons, screens, and controls translates into a safe and smooth journey for all on board.

Pilots are also the primary communicators for their aircraft, serving as the liaison between the ground and the air. This role requires impeccable communication skills, as they must convey critical information to air traffic controllers, respond to changing weather conditions, and coordinate with the cabin crew to maintain a secure and comfortable environment for passengers.

The modern airline pilot must be a quick thinker and a calm decision-maker. Amidst the routine flights, they are trained to handle unexpected events with composure and efficiency. Whether it's a technical malfunction or an emergency situation, pilots are equipped with the training and experience to navigate through challenges and bring their passengers safely to their destination.

In addition to their operational duties, pilots today are ambassadors of customer service. They represent the airline, and their interactions with passengers can shape the travel experience. From the welcoming announcement to the final goodbye, pilots have the opportunity to leave a lasting impression, one that reflects the values and professionalism of their career.

The evolution of aviation technology has also transformed the pilot's role. Autopilot systems and advanced navigation tools have shifted the focus from manual flying to system management and oversight. Pilots must be adept at understanding and operating these systems, all while maintaining the core flying skills that are the foundation of their profession.

Continuous education is a hallmark of an airline pilot's career. With the ever-changing landscape of aviation regulations, technology, and best practices, pilots are lifelong learners. They regularly undergo training and recertification to stay at the forefront of the industry, ensuring that their knowledge and skills are always up to date.

The airline pilot of today is also a team player, working closely with co-pilots, cabin crew, maintenance personnel, and ground staff to ensure a seamless operation. This collaborative environment is essential for maintaining the high standards of safety and efficiency that define commercial aviation.

As we journey through the day-to-day life of an airline pilot, we uncover a role that is as demanding as it is rewarding. It's a career that calls for discipline, precision, and a passion for flying. It's a profession that carries the responsibility of transporting people across the globe, connecting lives and fulfilling dreams.

The skies are a dynamic and ever-changing workplace, and airline pilots are the skilled professionals who navigate this realm. They are the ones who watch the sunrise at 35,000 feet, who fly above the clouds, and who experience the world from a perspective few can imagine.

2 / educational pathways

blueprints to the pilot's seat

THE JOURNEY to the pilot's seat is a structured and meticulous process, demanding a blend of academic rigor, practical training, and an unwavering commitment to excellence. The path is not merely a series of steps but a continuous ascent towards the pinnacle of aeronautical proficiency.

Embarking on this path requires a clear understanding of the educational framework and qualifications that form the backbone of a pilot's career. It begins with the foundational knowledge of physics and mathematics, subjects that are essential for grasping the principles of flight and aircraft operation. A strong grasp of these subjects is crucial, as they are the bedrock upon which all flying theory is built.

Prospective pilots often start their journey with a bachelor's degree in aviation, aerospace engineering, or a related field. These programs offer a comprehensive curriculum that covers a wide range of topics, from the basics of aerodynamics to the complexities of aviation law. However, a degree is not the only route into aviation; many successful pilots have taken alternative pathways, including military training or starting as an aviation mechanic.

Regardless of the educational background, all pilots must earn their wings through rigorous training and certification. The first step is obtaining a Private Pilot License (PPL), which allows one to fly small aircraft under visual flight rules. The PPL is the first significant milestone in a pilot's training, providing the foundational skills needed for all future flying.

The next step is the Commercial Pilot License (CPL), which requires additional flight hours, advanced training, and passing a series of written and practical exams. The CPL is the key that unlocks the door to professional flying, whether it's for charter operations, flight instruction, or as a stepping stone to an airline career.

For those aiming for the airlines, the Airline Transport Pilot License (ATPL) is the gold standard. It's the highest certification a pilot can achieve and requires meeting stringent requirements, including a minimum number of flight hours, passing comprehensive written exams, and demonstrating proficiency in a multi-crew environment.

Beyond licenses, pilots must also obtain type ratings for the specific aircraft they wish to fly. Each type rating involves detailed training on the systems, performance, and emergency procedures for that particular aircraft model. This specialization ensures that pilots are intimately familiar with the nuances of the machines they command.

The qualifications of a pilot are not limited to licenses and ratings. They must also pass rigorous medical examinations to ensure they are fit to fly. These exams assess a pilot's physical and mental health, as they must be able to perform under the demanding conditions of the cockpit.

In addition to formal qualifications, pilots must possess a set of soft skills that are just as critical. Communication, leadership, decision-making, and teamwork are all integral to the role of a pilot. They must be able to work harmoniously with a diverse crew, handle stress effectively, and make split-second decisions that could have far-reaching consequences.

The education and qualifications required to become a pilot are extensive, but they are designed to prepare individuals for the immense responsibility that comes with the role. It's a career that demands precision, dedication, and a lifelong commitment to learning and improvement.

As we navigate through the educational landscape of aviation, we gain a deeper appreciation for the level of expertise required to safely transport passengers across the skies. It's a testament to the professionalism and dedication of pilots, who undergo years of training to achieve their dreams.

navigating the flight path: a guide to aviation education

The pursuit of a career in aviation is an expedition that begins with a single step into the world of aviation schools and training programs. These institutions are not just buildings with runways and aircraft; they are gateways to the skies, where dreams of flight become reality.

Choosing the right aviation school or training program is a decision that sets the trajectory for one's future in the field. It's a place where aspiring pilots are forged through a combination of rigorous academics, hands-on experience, and the cultivation of a pilot's mindset. The environment is one of discipline and dedication, where every lesson is a building block towards a license to fly.

Aviation schools come in various forms, from university-affiliated programs offering degrees in aviation to independent flight schools focused solely on pilot training. Each has its unique advantages, catering to different learning styles and career goals. University programs often provide a broader educational experience, with courses in aviation management, safety, and even unmanned aerial systems, alongside pilot training.

Independent flight schools, on the other hand, offer a more concentrated curriculum, often allowing students to progress more quickly towards their flying goals. These schools vary widely in size, fleet, and facilities, but they share a common purpose: to equip students with the skills and knowledge necessary to succeed in the cockpit.

Training programs are meticulously structured, with each phase designed to build upon the last. Ground school lays the theoretical foundation, covering topics such as meteorology, navigation, and aerodynamics. This is where students learn the language of aviation, the principles that govern flight, and the regulations that ensure safety.

Flight training is where theory meets practice. Under the guidance of experienced instructors, students take to the air, learning to handle an aircraft through various maneuvers, conditions, and scenarios. It's a process that demands focus and precision, as students develop the muscle memory and decision-making skills that will define their piloting style.

Simulator training is another critical component, providing a risk-free environment to practice and perfect flying skills. Advanced simulators replicate the experience of flying various aircraft, allowing students to train for normal, abnormal, and emergency situations without ever leaving the ground.

The journey through aviation education is not a solitary one. It's a shared experience, with students and instructors working closely together, forming bonds that often last a lifetime. It's a community of like-minded individuals, all driven by a passion for aviation and a commitment to excellence.

As students progress through their training, they also develop a professional network that will support them throughout their careers. They learn from the experiences of their peers and instructors, gaining insights into the realities of a pilot's life.

The culmination of this education is a series of exams and check rides that test a student's knowledge and skills. Passing these is a rite of passage, marking the transition from student to pilot. It's a moment of immense pride and a milestone that opens the door to the world of professional flying.

Aviation education is an investment in the future, requiring time, effort, and resources. But for those who complete the journey, the rewards are immeasurable. It's not just about earning a license to fly; it's about joining a special fraternity of individuals who have mastered the art of aviation.

the academic and certification ladder in aviation

The world of aviation is one where precision meets passion, and where education and certification form the rungs of the ladder leading to the cockpit. For those who aspire to navigate the skies, understanding the academic and certification landscape is as crucial as learning to fly.

The academic journey for a pilot often begins with a bachelor's degree. While not mandatory, a degree in aviation provides a comprehensive foundation that covers all aspects of flight operations, as well as the business and management side of the industry. Programs typically include courses in meteorology, aerodynamics, and navigation, alongside general education requirements. These degrees are designed to not only educate but also to shape well-rounded professionals who understand the broader context of their role in the aviation ecosystem.

For many, the choice to pursue a degree is driven by the desire for a deeper understanding of the science behind aviation, as well as the potential for career advancement. Airlines often look favorably upon candidates with degrees, seeing them as individuals who have demonstrated a commitment to their field and who possess a breadth of knowledge that extends beyond the cockpit.

Parallel to academic pursuits are the certifications that are the lifeblood of a pilot's qualifications. The journey begins with the Private Pilot License (PPL), which serves as the entry point into the world of flying. It's the first official stamp of approval, the first nod from the aviation authorities that says, "Yes, you can fly."

But the PPL is just the beginning. The Commercial Pilot License (CPL) is where the dream of flying for a living starts to take shape. It's a more demanding process, with higher standards of proficiency and a greater number of flight hours required. The CPL is a significant achievement, a testament to a pilot's skills and their dedication to their craft.

The pinnacle of pilot certification is the Airline Transport Pilot License (ATPL), the highest level of pilot licensure. To sit for the ATPL exams, pilots must accumulate a substantial number of flight hours and demonstrate a mastery of a wide range of subjects, from flight planning to crew resource management. The ATPL is not just a license; it's a symbol of expertise, experience, and the highest level of trust bestowed upon a pilot.

Type ratings are another critical piece of the certification puzzle. Each type of aircraft has its own set of systems, performance characteristics, and emergency procedures, and pilots must be certified to fly each one.

Type ratings involve intensive training, both in the classroom and in simulators, culminating in a check ride that tests a pilot's ability to operate the aircraft under various conditions.

Beyond the formal certifications, there are numerous other qualifications that pilots can pursue to enhance their skills and marketability. These include instructor certifications, instrument ratings, and multi-engine ratings, each opening new doors and presenting new opportunities within the industry.

The path to becoming a pilot is one of continuous learning and development. It's a career where the learning never stops, where each flight is an opportunity to refine skills and where every simulator session is a chance to better prepare for the unexpected.

In the world of aviation, degrees and certifications are more than just pieces of paper. They are milestones, each marking a new level of achievement and a step closer to the ultimate goal of becoming a captain. They are the credentials that pilots carry with them, a record of their journey, and a promise of their commitment to safety and excellence.

3 / getting your wings

earning your wings: the journey to a private pilot license

THE JOURNEY to earning a Private Pilot License (PPL) is the first significant leap towards the skies for aspiring aviators. It's a chapter in one's life that unfolds with the promise of freedom, the thrill of solo flight, and the beginning of a lifelong romance with the heavens.

The PPL serves as the cornerstone of a pilot's education, a testament to their ability to command a single-engine aircraft with confidence and skill. It's a license that opens up new horizons, allowing pilots to share the magic of flight with friends and family, and to explore the world from a vantage point few can claim to know.

The process of obtaining a PPL is both rigorous and rewarding, designed to instill the fundamentals of flying while testing the resolve and dedication of the student. It begins with ground school, where one delves into the theoretical aspects of aviation. Here, students immerse themselves in subjects such as navigation, meteorology, and aircraft systems, laying the groundwork for what will come in the air.

Flight training is where the real adventure begins. It's where knowledge is put into practice, and where students experience the joy and challenge of piloting an aircraft. Under the watchful eye of an instructor, students learn to perform pre-flight inspections, handle takeoffs and landings, and navigate the airspace with precision.

The PPL curriculum is designed to build a pilot's skills progressively, starting with basic maneuvers and advancing to cross-country flights and emergency procedures. Each lesson is a step closer to the ultimate test of a pilot's abilities: the solo flight. This milestone is a rite of passage, a moment where the instructor steps out of the aircraft, and the student takes control, alone at the helm for the first time.

The solo flight is a transformative experience, one that marks the transition from student to pilot. It's a time of reflection, of understanding the weight of responsibility that comes with the title, and of immense personal achievement. It's a memory that will be cherished, a story that will be told and retold with pride.

As students progress through their training, they also

prepare for the written exam, a comprehensive test that covers all the ground school topics. It's an exam that requires diligence and study, but one that reinforces the knowledge essential for safe and competent flying.

The final step in the PPL journey is the check ride, an examination conducted by an FAA-designated pilot examiner. It's a day of nerves and excitement, where students must demonstrate their flying proficiency and decision-making skills. The check ride is the culmination of all the hard work, the early mornings, and the late-night study sessions. It's the moment where students earn their wings.

Obtaining a PPL is more than just acquiring the ability to fly; it's about embracing a new identity as a pilot. It's about joining a community of like-minded individuals who share a passion for aviation and a respect for the art of flying.

The PPL is also a foundation for further advancement in aviation. For some, it's a stepping stone to a Commercial Pilot License or even an Airline Transport Pilot License. For others, it's a ticket to a lifetime of recreational flying, exploring the skies, and experiencing the freedom that comes with being a pilot.

Roger Smith

ascending to new heights: the commercial pilot license

The Commercial Pilot License (CPL) represents a significant milestone in the career of a pilot, a beacon that signifies a readiness to embrace the responsibilities of commercial aviation. It's a journey that builds upon the foundation laid by the Private Pilot License (PPL), propelling pilots into the realm of professional flying.

The path to a CPL is one of dedication and discipline, where pilots refine their skills and expand their knowledge to meet the demands of the aviation industry. It's a transformative process that takes the raw potential of a private pilot and molds it into the caliber required for commercial operations.

The transition from PPL to CPL is marked by an increase in both the quantity and complexity of training. Flight hours accumulate, and with them, experience grows. Pilots learn to navigate not just the skies but also the intricacies of commercial flight operations. They become adept at flying in a variety of conditions, mastering instruments, and understanding the nuances of different aircraft.

Training for a CPL involves advanced flight maneuvers, complex navigation, and a deeper dive into the operational aspects of flying. Pilots learn about the economics of aviation, the principles of crew resource management, and the importance of operational planning. They are trained to think like captains, to anticipate needs, and to manage resources efficiently.

The coursework for a CPL candidate is rigorous, covering topics such as advanced meteorology, high-performance aircraft systems, and the regulatory framework governing commercial flight. The theoretical knowledge gained is not merely academic; it's practical, applicable, and vital for the safe operation of commercial flights.

One of the hallmarks of CPL training is the emphasis on decision-making and judgment. Pilots are taught to evaluate situations critically, to weigh risks, and to make decisions that prioritize safety above all else. They learn to balance the pressures of commercial operations with the unforgiving realities of physics and weather.

The flight training for a CPL is comprehensive, covering cross-country flying, night operations, and multi-engine aircraft handling. Each flight is an opportunity to hone skills, to practice the art of airmanship, and to prepare for the unexpected. Instructors push students to excel, to fly with precision, and to command the aircraft with authority.

The culmination of CPL training is the check ride, a rigorous examination that tests a pilot's ability to perform under pressure. It's an assessment of not just flying skills but also of a pilot's judgment, situational awareness, and ability to operate within the commercial aviation environment.

Earning a CPL is not the end of the journey; it's a new beginning. It opens doors to career opportunities, from instructing new pilots to flying charter flights or even joining an airline. The CPL is a passport to a world of professional flying, a credential that speaks to a pilot's skills, knowledge, and professionalism.

The journey to a CPL is as challenging as it is rewarding. It requires a commitment to continuous learning, a dedication to excellence, and a passion for flying. It's a path that demands the best of those who choose to walk it, and in return, it offers a career that is dynamic, fulfilling, and full of possibilities.

As pilots embark on the journey to a CPL, they do so with the knowledge that they are not just learning to fly; they are learning to lead. They are becoming the pilots who will carry passengers safely to their destinations, who will navigate the complexities of the skies, and who will uphold the highest standards of the aviation profession.

the captain's journey: mastering the airline transport pilot license

The Airline Transport Pilot License (ATPL) stands as the zenith of a pilot's certification journey, a beacon of the highest standard in aviation expertise. It is the license that crowns a pilot as a captain, ready to take command of commercial airliners and navigate the complex airspace of the world's busiest routes.

The ATPL is not merely a step up from the Commercial Pilot License (CPL); it is a quantum leap in responsibility, knowledge, and skill. It is the culmination of years of training, flying, and learning, a testament to a pilot's unwavering commitment to the craft of aviation.

The road to an ATPL is paved with advanced theoretical knowledge and practical experience. Pilots must immerse themselves in subjects that delve into the intricacies of air law, aircraft performance, operational procedures, and human factors. The depth of study is profound, covering the minutiae of flight planning, the complexities of international regulations, and the subtleties of crew coordination.

Flight hours are the currency of a pilot's experience, and for the ATPL, the ledger must be rich with diverse entries. Pilots must accrue significant time in the air, demonstrating their ability to command multi-crew aircraft and handle a variety of operational challenges. Each flight hour is a building block, adding to a foundation robust enough to support the weight of a captain's stripes.

The practical component of ATPL training is equally demanding. Pilots must prove their proficiency in high-fidelity simulators, replicating the most challenging conditions they are likely to face in the cockpit. These sessions test a pilot's mettle, honing their decision-making, problem-solving, and leadership abilities under pressure.

The ATPL exams are a formidable challenge, designed to ensure that only those with the requisite knowledge and judgment can lead a commercial flight. The exams cover a broad spectrum of topics, each one critical to the safe and efficient operation of modern airliners. Passing these exams is a rite of passage, marking a pilot's transition from first officer to captain.

But the ATPL is more than a series of tests and logged hours; it is a symbol of trust. It signifies that a pilot is trusted by regulators, airlines, and passengers to safely navigate not just an aircraft, but also the lives and hopes of those on board. It is a trust earned through dedication, skill, and an unwavering commitment to excellence.

The ATPL also opens the door to leadership opportunities within the aviation industry. Captains are not just pilots; they are mentors, instructors, and role models. They carry the responsibility of guiding the next generation of pilots, sharing their knowledge, and shaping the future of aviation.

The journey to an ATPL is as rewarding as it is rigorous. It is a path that offers the chance to see the world, to connect cultures, and to be part of an industry that is at the forefront of technology and innovation. It is a career that demands the best and, in return, offers a sense of accomplishment that few professions can match.

As pilots embark on the ATPL journey, they do so with the knowledge that they are striving for the pinnacle of their profession. They are pursuing a license that is recognized and respected around the globe, a credential that speaks to their expertise and their readiness to lead.

4 /
building experience

chronicles of the sky: the pilot's logbook

IN THE LIFE OF A PILOT, the logbook is more than a collection of pages; it's a chronicle of journeys, a ledger of growth, and a legal document that bears witness to the evolution of an aviator. Each entry is a story, a testament to the experiences that shape a pilot's career, and a key that unlocks the doors to new opportunities and horizons.

The logbook is the pilot's constant companion, a meticulous record of flight hours, destinations, aircraft types, maneuvers, and conditions. It's a reflection of dedication, a narrative of challenges met and overcome, and a portfolio of the skills honed over countless hours spent in the cockpit.

For aspiring pilots, the logbook begins with the first

entry, the first time they take the controls and feel the aircraft respond. It's a moment of profound significance, the start of a journey that will take them to the far reaches of the sky and the depths of their own capabilities.

As pilots progress through their training, the logbook grows, each entry building upon the last. It's a tangible measure of their advancement, from student to private pilot, from private pilot to commercial aviator, and perhaps, one day, to the captain of an airliner.

Flight hours are the currency of a pilot's progression, each one carefully logged, categorized, and endorsed. There are hours of dual instruction, where the wisdom of experienced pilots is imparted. There are solo hours, where the pilot's own judgment and skill are the sole guides. There are instrument hours, night hours, and cross-country hours, each with its own lessons and rewards.

The logbook is also a legal requirement, a document that must be presented for examination during check rides, interviews, and regulatory audits. It's a record that must be kept with precision and care, for it not only charts a pilot's past but also paves the way for their future.

In the commercial realm, the logbook serves as a resume, a detailed account of a pilot's experience and qualifications. Airlines scrutinize logbooks, looking for the breadth and depth of experience that will ensure their aircraft and passengers are in capable hands.

Beyond its practical applications, the logbook is a personal journal, a collection of memories that pilots cherish. It's a reminder of the places they've seen, the people they've met, and the aircraft they've flown. It's a record of sunrises and sunsets witnessed from above the clouds, of storms navigated and clear skies savored.

The act of logging hours is a discipline in itself, a ritual that instills attention to detail and an appreciation for the journey. Each entry is a reflection, an opportunity to consider the flight just completed, to learn from it, and to carry those lessons forward.

For pilots, the logbook is a source of pride, a testament to their commitment and passion for flying. It's a record that speaks to the hours of hard work, the sacrifices made, and the dreams realized. It's a narrative of personal achievement, a story that is uniquely theirs.

As pilots close their logbooks at the end of each flight, they do so with the knowledge that they are contributing to a legacy, a history of aviation that stretches back to the first pioneers of the sky. They are part of a continuum, a lineage of aviators who have charted the unknown and brought the world closer together.

mentorship in the skies: the role of flight instructors

The role of a flight instructor is pivotal in the aviation industry, serving as the bridge between the academic world and the practical realm of flying. Instructors are the seasoned guides who shepherd new pilots through the complexities of aviation, imparting wisdom and fostering the skills necessary for students to thrive in the skies.

Flight instructors come from a variety of backgrounds, but they all share a common thread: a deep knowledge of aviation and a passion for teaching. They are the custodians of flight safety, the architects of a student's confidence, and the catalysts for turning aspirations into reality.

The journey to becoming a flight instructor is itself a rigorous process, requiring a thorough understanding of educational methodologies, flight regulations, and the nuances of different aircraft. Instructors must be adept communicators, capable of breaking down complex concepts into digestible lessons that resonate with students of all levels.

In the cockpit, instructors are both teachers and guardians. They monitor their students' progress, providing real-time feedback and correction. They create scenarios that challenge and stretch their pupils, preparing them for the unpredictable nature of flying. It's a role that demands patience, adaptability, and an unwavering commitment to excellence.

For many pilots, the role of an instructor is also a means of building flight hours. While instructing, they accumulate the precious time needed to advance their own careers, often towards the goal of flying for commercial airlines. Each hour logged is dual-purpose, enhancing their experience while shaping the next generation of aviators.

The relationship between instructor and student is a dynamic one, built on trust and mutual respect. Instructors must balance encouragement with discipline, ensuring that students not only learn but also understand the gravity of the responsibility they will carry as pilots.

Instructors also play a critical role in the safety culture of aviation. They instill best practices, emphasize the importance of pre-flight checks, and teach risk management strategies. They are the first line of defense in preventing accidents, equipping their students with the mindset and skills to navigate safely through both clear and turbulent skies.

The time-building phase for pilots is an investment in their future. It's a period of honing skills, expanding knowledge, and solidifying the habits that will define their approach to flying. It's a time when pilots learn not just to fly but to excel, pushing the boundaries of their abilities and striving for the precision that aviation demands.

As instructors mold their students, they also refine their own skills. Teaching is a reciprocal process, one that benefits both the mentor and the mentee. Instructors find their own understanding deepened through the act of teaching, and their proficiency sharpened by the challenges of instructing.

The chapter of instructor roles and time building is a foundational one in the story of a pilot's career. It's a chapter that shapes the future of aviation, one flight lesson at a time. It's a narrative of growth, challenge, and the relentless pursuit of mastery in the art of flying.

For those who take on the mantle of flight instructor, the rewards are manifold. They experience the satisfaction of guiding students to success, the joy of sharing their love of flying, and the pride of contributing to the legacy of aviation safety and education.

taking flight: regional airlines as career launchpads

The ascent through the ranks of aviation often begins with the regional airlines, those smaller carriers that operate shorter routes but play a colossal role in the career development of pilots. For many aviators, these airlines are not just employers; they are the crucibles where skills are refined, confidence is built, and professional identities are forged.

Regional airlines serve as the proving grounds for pilots, offering a unique blend of opportunities and challenges that prepare them for the larger stages of their careers. It's here that pilots transition from the theoretical knowledge of flight school to the practical realities of commercial aviation.

The experience gained at a regional airline is invaluable. Pilots learn to operate in the commercial environment, adhering to tight schedules, managing diverse crews, and ensuring passenger satisfaction. They become adept at navigating complex airspaces, communicating with busy control towers, and handling the operational pressures that come with commercial flights.

For pilots, regional airlines offer a more accessible entry point into the industry. The flight hour requirements for first officers are often lower than those at major carriers, allowing pilots to build their careers from the ground up. It's a chance to gain the experience needed to meet the stringent requirements of major airlines, all while earning a living and honing their craft.

The cockpit of a regional airliner is a classroom without walls. Every flight is a lesson in meteorology, airmanship, and problem-solving. Pilots learn to contend with adverse weather, equipment malfunctions, and the unexpected events that are part and parcel of flying. It's an environment that demands quick thinking, clear communication, and decisive action.

The camaraderie among regional airline pilots is another cornerstone of the experience. These pilots often share a common goal: to advance to larger airlines and more complex aircraft. This shared ambition fosters a supportive atmosphere where knowledge is exchanged, advice is given, and friendships are formed.

Regional airlines also offer pilots the opportunity to quickly advance to the role of captain. The accelerated career progression is a double-edged sword, offering rapid advancement but also demanding a level of readiness and maturity that must match the responsibility of the left seat.

The role of captain at a regional airline is a significant milestone. It's a leadership position that requires not just flying expertise but also the ability to manage a crew, communicate effectively with passengers, and make critical decisions that impact the safety and efficiency of every flight.

The journey with regional airlines is a chapter filled with growth. Pilots expand their professional network, encounter a variety of operational environments, and develop the leadership qualities that are essential for their future roles. They emerge from this experience not just as pilots who can fly an aircraft but as aviation professionals who can navigate the complexities of the industry.

As pilots look back on their time with regional airlines, they often do so with gratitude. These carriers were the launchpads for their careers, the places where they transformed from students of aviation into its practitioners. The hours logged, the flights commanded, and the challenges overcome during this time are the foundation upon which successful aviation careers are built.

The narrative of regional airlines in a pilot's career is one of beginnings. It's the start of a professional journey, a chapter where the seeds of future success are sown. It's a time of learning, of experience, and of preparation for the opportunities that lie ahead.

5 / the hiring process

clearing the runway: understanding airline application requirements

EMBARKING on a career with an airline is akin to preparing for a complex flight plan. It requires meticulous preparation, a clear understanding of the requirements, and a strategy to navigate the application process successfully. For pilots, the application to an airline is the culmination of years of hard work, training, and dedication to their craft.

The airline application process is multifaceted, encompassing a range of requirements that go beyond flight hours and certifications. Airlines are looking for candidates who not only meet the technical qualifications but also embody the professional and personal attributes that align with their culture and values.

Flight Experience and Certifications

At the core of the application requirements are the pilot's flight experience and certifications. Airlines typically specify a minimum number of flight hours, often broken down into categories such as Pilot-in-Command (PIC) time, multi-engine time, and instrument flight rules (IFR) hours. These requirements ensure that pilots have the practical experience necessary to operate commercial flights safely.

In addition to flight hours, airlines require pilots to hold certain certifications. The Airline Transport Pilot License (ATPL) is usually a prerequisite for captains, while first officers may be required to have at least a Commercial Pilot License (CPL) with an instrument rating. Type ratings for specific aircraft may also be required or preferred, depending on the airline's fleet.

Educational Background

While not always mandatory, a bachelor's degree is increasingly becoming a standard requirement for airline pilots. Degrees in aviation, aerospace engineering, or related fields are common, but airlines also value degrees that demonstrate critical thinking, problem-solving, and communication skills.

Medical Fitness

Pilots must maintain a valid first-class medical certificate to ensure they meet the health and fitness standards required for commercial flying. This includes regular medical examinations that assess a pilot's physical and mental health.

Skills and Attributes

Beyond the technical qualifications, airlines seek pilots with a suite of soft skills and personal attributes. Leadership, decision-making, teamwork, and communication skills are critical in the cockpit. Airlines also look for candidates who demonstrate adaptability, situational awareness, and a commitment to continuous learning.

Background Checks and Security Clearances

Given the nature of the job, pilots undergo thorough background checks. This includes scrutiny of their criminal record, employment history, and references. Security clearances are also a requirement, particularly for airlines that operate international routes.

Preparation for Assessments

The application process often involves assessments that can include aptitude tests, simulator evaluations, and interviews. Pilots must prepare for these assessments by reviewing technical knowledge, practicing in simulators, and honing their interview skills.

Application and Interview Process

The application itself must be approached with care. Pilots should ensure their resumes are up-to-date, highlighting relevant experience and qualifications. Cover letters should be tailored to the airline, demonstrating an understanding of the company's operations and culture.

During interviews, pilots have the opportunity to showcase their knowledge, experience, and passion for aviation. They should be prepared to discuss their logbooks, answer technical questions, and provide examples of how they have handled challenging situations in the past.

Cultural Fit and Company Research

Understanding the culture of the airline and how one's personal values align with it is crucial. Researching the airline's history, mission, and operations can provide insights that help candidates present themselves as a good fit for the company.

Networking and Professional Development

Building a professional network within the industry can provide valuable insights and opportunities. Attending aviation conferences, joining professional organizations, and connecting with current airline employees can open doors and offer guidance through the application process.

The path to securing a position with an airline is competitive and demanding. It requires a comprehensive approach that balances technical proficiency with personal development. For pilots, each step of the application process is an opportunity to demonstrate their readiness to take on the responsibilities of commercial flight.

As pilots navigate the application requirements, they

do so with the knowledge that they are seeking to join a profession that is not just a job but a lifestyle. It's a career that offers the chance to travel the world, connect with diverse cultures, and be part of an industry that is at the forefront of technology and innovation.

the final approach: mastering the airline interview and selection process

The journey to becoming an airline pilot is punctuated by one critical milestone: the interview and selection process. It's the final approach to a coveted position in the cockpit, a stage where preparation meets opportunity, and where aspiring pilots must shine.

The interview process is a multifaceted assessment that evaluates a candidate's technical knowledge, psychological readiness, and cultural fit within the airline. It's an opportunity for airlines to look beyond the logbook and certifications, to see the person behind the pilot.

Technical Assessments

The first hurdle often involves technical assessments. These can range from written exams testing aeronautical knowledge to simulator sessions evaluating a pilot's flying skills. Candidates must demonstrate a deep understanding of aviation principles, aircraft systems, and emergency procedures. It's a test of their ability to apply theoretical knowledge in practical scenarios.

Psychometric Testing

Psychometric testing is another component of the selection process. These tests measure cognitive abilities, personality traits, and situational judgment. They are designed to ensure that pilots possess the mental agility, emotional stability, and decision-making skills necessary for the demands of commercial aviation.

Group Exercises and Interviews

Group exercises are commonly used to assess teamwork and communication skills. Candidates may be asked to solve problems collaboratively or participate in role-playing scenarios. These exercises reveal how pilots interact with others, manage conflict, and contribute to a team's success.

The personal interview is a critical phase where candidates engage directly with airline representatives. It's a chance to convey passion for aviation, to discuss career aspirations, and demonstrate how one's experiences align with the airline's values and objectives.

Scenario-Based Questions

Interviewers often employ scenario-based questions to evaluate a pilot's judgment and problem-solving abilities. Candidates must articulate how they would handle various flight situations, showcasing their capacity to think on their feet and make sound decisions under pressure.

Cultural Fit and Company Values

Understanding the airline's culture and values is essential. Candidates should research the airline's history, mission, and operational philosophy. This knowledge allows them to tailor their responses to resonate with the company's ethos and to present themselves as a natural fit for the team.

Preparation and Practice

Preparation is key to navigating the interview process successfully. This includes reviewing technical materials, practicing for psychometric tests, and rehearsing for interviews. Candidates should also reflect on their experiences, identifying examples that demonstrate their competencies and readiness for the role.

Feedback and Reflection

Feedback from the interview process, whether positive or negative, is invaluable. It provides insights into areas of strength and opportunities for improvement. Reflecting on the experience allows candidates to refine their approach and enhance their prospects for future opportunities.

Professionalism and Presentation

Throughout the selection process, professionalism is paramount. This extends to attire, demeanor, and communication. First impressions matter, and candidates must present themselves as polished professionals who are ready to represent the airline.

Networking and Mentorship

Networking with industry professionals and seeking mentorship can provide guidance and support. Engaging with current airline pilots and industry experts can offer insider perspectives on the interview process and tips for success.

Resilience and Persistence

The path to an airline cockpit is competitive, and not all candidates will succeed on their first attempt. Resilience and persistence are vital traits for pilots. The determination to learn from each experience and to persist in the face of setbacks is often what separates successful candidates from the rest.

The airline interview and selection process is the gateway to a career in the skies. It's a comprehensive evaluation that tests a pilot's abilities, character, and fit within the airline. For those who navigate it successfully, it marks the beginning of a new chapter, one filled with the promise of adventure, the fulfillment of dreams, and the honor of flying the friendly skies.

the art of simulation: a pilot's guide to simulator assessments

In the world of aviation, the simulator is an invaluable tool, a realm where pilots can hone their skills, confront their fears, and prepare for the unexpected without ever leaving the ground. Simulator assessments are a critical component of a pilot's journey, serving as both a test of their abilities and a crucible for their development.

These assessments are not mere formalities; they are comprehensive evaluations of a pilot's competence, decision-making, and ability to handle adverse situations. They are designed to replicate the pressures of real-world flying, providing a safe environment to make mistakes and learn from them.

The Role of Simulators in Pilot Training

Simulators play a pivotal role in pilot training, offering an immersive experience that mirrors the complexities of an actual cockpit. From the hum of the engines to the visual display of the terrain, every detail is meticulously recreated to provide a realistic flying experience.

For pilots, the simulator is both a classroom and a laboratory. It's a place where they can practice maneuvers, experiment with different flight conditions, and perfect their responses to emergencies. The feedback received is immediate and precise, allowing for targeted improvements and a deeper understanding of the aircraft's behavior.

Preparing for Simulator Assessments

Preparation for simulator assessments is as much mental as it is technical. Pilots must enter the simulator with a clear mind, a thorough knowledge of the aircraft, and a strategy for managing the scenarios they will face. This preparation involves studying the aircraft's systems, reviewing standard operating procedures, and mentally rehearsing the tasks ahead.

Assessment Scenarios

During the assessment, pilots are presented with a variety of scenarios, each carefully crafted to evaluate specific skills. These may include engine failures, hydraulic malfunctions, or navigational challenges. The scenarios test a pilot's ability to remain calm under pressure, to prioritize tasks, and to maintain situational awareness.

Performance Metrics

The metrics used to evaluate performance in a simulator are diverse. They include technical proficiency, adherence to procedures, and the quality of decision-making. Instructors and examiners look for smoothness of control inputs, efficiency of cockpit management, and the ability to anticipate and mitigate risks.

Feedback and Debriefing

A critical aspect of simulator assessments is the

debriefing session that follows. It's a time for reflection and learning, where instructors provide feedback on the pilot's performance. The debriefing focuses on areas of strength, identifies areas for improvement, and discusses strategies for addressing any weaknesses.

The Psychological Aspect

Simulator assessments also have a psychological dimension. They are designed to induce stress, mimicking the emotional responses pilots may experience in real flight. How pilots manage this stress, maintain composure, and perform their duties is a key aspect of the assessment.

Continuous Learning

The simulator is a tool for continuous learning, a place where pilots can return time and again to refine their skills. The lessons learned within its confines are directly transferable to the aircraft, making simulator assessments an integral part of a pilot's ongoing professional development.

The Future of Simulation

As technology advances, so too do the capabilities of simulators. They are becoming increasingly sophisticated, offering higher levels of realism and new opportunities for training. The future of simulation is one of endless possibilities, where virtual reality and artificial intelligence will further enhance the training experience.

6 / life in the cockpit

the dynamics of airline operations: a comprehensive overview

AIRLINE OPERATIONS ARE the heartbeat of the aviation industry, a complex symphony of processes, people, and technology that come together to transport passengers and cargo across the globe. Understanding these operations is crucial for any aviation professional, as it provides insight into the multifaceted nature of flying beyond the cockpit.

The Essence of Airline Operations

At its core, airline operations encompass everything from flight planning and crew scheduling to maintenance and customer service. It's a vast ecosystem that relies on precision, efficiency, and coordination to succeed. Every flight is the result of meticulous planning and execution, with countless professionals working behind the scenes to ensure safety and punctuality.

Flight Planning and Dispatch

Flight planning is where each journey begins. Dispatchers and pilots collaborate to chart the course, considering factors such as weather, air traffic, and fuel requirements. The flight plan is a document that outlines the route, altitude, and speed, ensuring the aircraft navigates the skies safely and efficiently.

Crew Scheduling and Management

Crew scheduling is a complex puzzle that airlines must solve daily. Pilots and cabin crew must be assigned to flights in a way that adheres to regulatory requirements, maximizes efficiency, and considers individual work limits. Crew management systems are essential tools that help airlines keep track of qualifications, availability, and duty times.

Aircraft Maintenance and Safety

Aircraft maintenance is the cornerstone of airline operations. Regular inspections, repairs, and overhauls are conducted to keep the fleet airworthy. Maintenance teams work around the clock to address any issues, following strict protocols to ensure that every aircraft meets the highest safety standards.

Ground Operations

Ground operations are critical to the turnaround process. This includes baggage handling, refueling, catering, and boarding. Each task must be synchronized to minimize delays and provide a seamless experience for passengers. Ground crews are the unsung heroes who keep the wheels of the airline turning.

Air Traffic Control and Coordination

Air traffic control (ATC) is an integral part of airline operations, guiding aircraft through the skies and managing the flow of traffic. Pilots and ATC officers must communicate effectively to maintain safe separation between aircraft and to navigate busy airspaces.

Customer Service and Experience

Customer service is the face of the airline, the direct link between the carrier and its passengers. From check-in agents to flight attendants, every interaction shapes the passenger experience. Airlines invest heavily in training staff to provide exceptional service, recognizing that customer satisfaction is key to their success.

Technology and Innovation

Technology is transforming airline operations, making them more efficient and responsive. From advanced booking systems to real-time tracking apps, airlines are embracing digital solutions to enhance their operations and to offer passengers more control over their travel experience.

Crisis Management and Contingency Planning

Crisis management is an inevitable part of airline operations. Whether it's a mechanical issue, a weather disruption, or an unexpected event, airlines must have contingency plans in place. Effective crisis management involves clear communication, swift decision-making, and a focus on safety above all else.

Environmental Considerations

Airlines are increasingly aware of their environmental impact and are taking steps to operate more sustainably. This includes investing in fuel-efficient aircraft, optimizing flight paths, and exploring alternative fuels. Environmental stewardship is becoming a priority, as airlines seek to balance operational demands with ecological responsibility.

Regulatory Compliance

Regulatory compliance is non-negotiable in airline operations. Airlines must adhere to a complex web of international and domestic regulations that govern every aspect of their operations. Compliance ensures that airlines maintain the trust of regulators, passengers, and the public.

The Future of Airline Operations

The future of airline operations is one of continuous improvement and adaptation. As the industry evolves, airlines must stay ahead of the curve, embracing new technologies, refining their processes, and meeting the changing needs of passengers.

Navigating the Complex World of Airline Operations

Understanding airline operations is essential for any

aviation professional. It provides a holistic view of the industry and highlights the interconnectivity of various roles. For pilots, a deep appreciation of airline operations enhances their ability to contribute to the airline's success and to deliver a safe, pleasant, and efficient travel experience.

navigating the skies: the pilot's role in modern aviation

The role of a pilot extends far beyond the act of flying. It encompasses a broad spectrum of responsibilities and duties that are critical to the safety, efficiency, and reliability of airline operations. Pilots are the linchpins of the aviation industry, entrusted with the lives of passengers and the integrity of the aircraft they command.

A Multifaceted Mandate

Pilots are not just aviators; they are leaders, decision-makers, and ambassadors of their airlines. They must possess a deep understanding of their aircraft, a comprehensive knowledge of the regulations that govern their operations, and the ability to interact with a diverse team of professionals both in the air and on the ground.

Safety as a Paramount Priority

The primary responsibility of a pilot is to ensure the safety of the flight. This duty begins well before takeoff, with thorough pre-flight checks and continues until the aircraft is safely parked at the gate. Pilots must be vigilant, always prepared to respond to any situation that may arise during the flight.

Mastery of the Machine

Pilots must have an intimate knowledge of the aircraft they operate. They need to understand its systems, capabilities, and limitations. This knowledge allows them to make informed decisions, whether it's navigating through turbulent weather or handling a technical malfunction.

Navigational Experts

Modern pilots are navigational experts, skilled in plotting courses that are both efficient and safe. They must be adept at using advanced avionics and navigation systems, ensuring that the aircraft remains on the planned route and arrives at its destination on schedule.

Communication is Key

Effective communication is a cornerstone of a pilot's responsibilities. This includes clear and concise interactions with air traffic control, as well as maintaining an open line of communication with the cabin crew and passengers. In times of delay or disruption, a pilot's ability to communicate effectively can greatly influence the passenger experience.

The Human Factor

Pilots must also manage the human factor, leading their crew with confidence and authority. They are responsible for fostering a professional environment where teamwork and cooperation are paramount. This leadership is crucial in maintaining high morale and ensuring that all crew members perform their roles effectively.

Continual Learning and Adaptation

The aviation industry is dynamic, with continuous advancements in technology and changes in regulations. Pilots must be committed to lifelong learning, regularly updating their skills and knowledge to stay abreast of new developments.

Environmental Stewardship

Pilots also play a role in environmental stewardship. They are tasked with operating the aircraft in a manner that minimizes fuel consumption and emissions, contributing to the airline's sustainability efforts.

Crisis Management

In the event of an emergency, pilots are the first line of response. They must remain calm, assess the situation, and execute the appropriate procedures to safeguard the aircraft and its occupants. Their actions in these critical moments can mean the difference between a close call and a catastrophe.

The Regulatory Landscape

Pilots must navigate the complex regulatory landscape of aviation, ensuring compliance with all laws and regulations. This includes staying current with licensing requirements, adhering to flight and duty time limitations, and maintaining the necessary medical fitness.

The Ambassadorial Role

Finally, pilots serve as ambassadors for their airlines. They represent the company's brand and values, and their interactions with passengers can significantly impact the airline's reputation.

sunrise to sunset: the pilot's journey

The life of an airline pilot is one of routine and adventure, structure and spontaneity, grounded in discipline yet soaring with freedom. It's a life that begins before dawn and stretches beyond the last light of day, a life where each day is both familiar and new.

Morning's First Light

A pilot's day starts early, often before the sun peeks over the horizon. The morning ritual is one of quiet preparation, a time for pilots to review their flight plans, check weather reports, and mentally prepare for the day ahead. A strong cup of coffee often accompanies a review of NOTAMs (Notices to Airmen) and a glance at the day's schedule.

Pre-Flight Preparations

Arriving at the airport, the world is already bustling. Pilots step into the operations center, a hub of activity where the day's logistics unfold. Here, they meet with their crew, discuss the flight plan, and address any concerns. The pre-flight briefing is thorough, covering everything from fuel loads to passenger counts.

The Walk-Around

With the briefing complete, pilots head to their aircraft, their steps purposeful, their minds focused. The walk-around inspection is a sacred ritual, a time-honored tradition where pilots become intimately acquainted with their aircraft. They check the wings, the engines, the fuselage, ensuring everything is as it should be.

Climbing into the Cockpit

Strapping into the cockpit, pilots are greeted by a symphony of screens and switches. They run through their checklists with precision, each action deliberate, each system checked and double-checked. The cockpit is their domain, a place of control and command.

Takeoff: The Thrill of Flight

As the engines roar to life, there's a palpable sense of anticipation. The takeoff is a moment of pure exhilaration, a dance between pilot and machine that never loses its thrill. The world falls away as the aircraft climbs, and the pilot's view is replaced by an expanse of blue.

The Dance with the Skies

Aloft, pilots navigate the skies with grace. They converse with air traffic control, adjust to changing weather patterns, and monitor their instruments. The flight deck is a place of constant vigilance, but also of unparalleled views—mountains, oceans, and cities passing below.

The In-Flight Ballet

Throughout the flight, pilots remain attuned to their aircraft and their environment. They manage the autopilot, communicate with the cabin crew, and provide updates to passengers. It's a ballet of tasks that keeps the flight smooth and the passengers comfortable.

Descent and Landing: A Return to Earth

As the journey nears its end, pilots prepare for descent. The approach is methodical, a careful orchestration of speed, altitude, and direction. The landing is the final act, a testament to the pilot's skill, as the aircraft touches down and the journey reaches its conclusion.

Post-Flight Reflections

With the engines quiet and the passengers disembarked, pilots conduct post-flight checks. They debrief with the crew, discuss any issues that arose, and complete their paperwork. It's a time of reflection, of lessons learned and experiences gained.

Rest and Rejuvenation

After a long day, pilots retreat from the world of runways and radar. They rest, recharge, and reconnect with life on the ground. Whether it's a night in a foreign city or a return home to loved ones, they savor the moments of stillness.

The Cycle Continues

The life of an airline pilot is cyclical, a pattern of departures and arrivals, of early mornings and late nights. But within this cycle lies a world of experiences, a career that is as challenging as it is rewarding, and a role that is vital to the fabric of modern life.

7 /
advanced training and certifications

mastering the machines: the journey through type ratings

THE LIFEBLOOD of an airline pilot's career is not just the ability to fly, but to fly a variety of aircraft. Each type of aircraft, with its unique systems, performance characteristics, and handling quirks, requires a specialized set of skills and knowledge. This is where type ratings come into play, serving as the pilot's passport to commanding different classes of airliners.

The Foundation of Flight

Type ratings are specialized training programs that certify a pilot to operate a specific aircraft type. They are the industry's acknowledgment that while the principles of flight remain constant, the specifics can vary dramatically from one cockpit to another.

Tailored Training for Each Type

The journey to earn a type rating begins with ground school, where pilots immerse themselves in the technical details of the aircraft. They study its avionics, engines, emergency procedures, and weight and balance calculations. This academic phase lays the groundwork for what comes next.

Simulator Sessions: Virtual Reality, Real Skills

After ground school, pilots step into the world of simulators. These high-fidelity machines replicate the aircraft's flight deck to perfection, providing a realistic and safe environment to practice. Pilots learn to handle normal and abnormal situations, from engine fires to instrument failures, honing their skills until responses become second nature.

The Check Ride: Proving Your Mettle

The culmination of type rating training is the check ride. It's a day of reckoning where pilots must demonstrate their mastery of the aircraft to an examiner. They are tested on their ability to manage the aircraft through a series of scenarios, proving they can do so safely and competently.

Beyond the Check Ride

Earning a type rating is not the end of learning. Pilots must engage in continuous training, refreshing their skills and staying current with any changes to the aircraft or its systems. This commitment to lifelong learning is a hallmark of the profession.

The Role of Type Ratings in Career Progression

Type ratings are more than just certifications; they are key milestones in a pilot's career progression. They open doors to new opportunities, allowing pilots to transition to larger, more complex aircraft as they advance.

The Impact on Airline Operations

For airlines, pilots with multiple type ratings offer flexibility in scheduling and fleet management. They can deploy these pilots across different routes and aircraft types, optimizing their operations and responding to the dynamic nature of the industry.

The Global Language of Type Ratings

Type ratings are recognized internationally, making them a global currency in the aviation job market. A pilot with a type rating for a widely used aircraft like the Boeing 737 or Airbus A320 is in high demand, able to work for airlines around the world.

The Personal and Professional Rewards

For pilots, type ratings are badges of honor. They represent the challenges overcome and the skills acquired. Each new type rating is a testament to a pilot's dedication and passion for flying.

The Future of Type Ratings

As aviation technology evolves, so too do type

ratings. Pilots must adapt to new advancements, such as glass cockpits and fly-by-wire systems. The type rating process will continue to evolve, incorporating new training methods and technologies to prepare pilots for the aircraft of tomorrow.

Type ratings are the building blocks of an airline pilot's career. They represent the specialized training and expertise required to command the diverse aircraft that crisscross our skies. For pilots, each type rating is a step forward in their journey, a new chapter in their ongoing story of flight.

elevating expertise: the cycle of recurrent training and checks

In the dynamic realm of aviation, the only constant is change. Pilots navigate this ever-shifting landscape through recurrent training and checks, a cyclical process that ensures their skills remain sharp and their knowledge up to date. This chapter delves into the ongoing journey of professional development that pilots undertake to maintain their edge in the skies.

The Pulse of Proficiency

Recurrent training is the pulse that keeps a pilot's proficiency alive. It's an ongoing commitment to excellence that transcends the initial type ratings and certifications. This training encompasses a broad spectrum of activities, from classroom instruction and online courses to simulator sessions and in-flight assessments.

Simulator Sessions: The Crucible of Competence

Simulators are the crucibles where pilots return regularly to refine their craft. Here, they encounter a range of scenarios designed to test their mettle—from engine failures at critical moments to complex system malfunctions. These sessions are not just about reinforcing routine operations; they're about preparing for the unexpected, ensuring pilots can handle any emergency with composure and skill.

Classroom Learning: The Theoretical Backbone

The theoretical backbone of recurrent training is found in the classroom. Pilots revisit the fundamentals of aerodynamics, meteorology, air law, and more. They delve into new regulations, emerging technologies, and best practices. This continuous learning environment fosters a culture of inquiry and adaptation, crucial traits for any aviator.

In-Flight Checks: The Reality Check

In-flight checks are the reality checks for pilots, where they demonstrate their flying abilities in the real world. Check pilots observe and evaluate, providing feedback that is both affirming and constructive. These checks are not about catching errors but about reinforcing excellence and encouraging growth.

The Annual Review: A Time for Reflection

The annual review is a time for reflection and evaluation. Pilots look back on their performance, celebrate their successes, and set goals for the year ahead. It's a holistic appraisal that considers not just technical skills but also aspects of leadership, communication, and teamwork.

The Role of Regulatory Bodies

Regulatory bodies play a pivotal role in shaping the recurrent training landscape. They set the standards, mandate the minimum requirements, and audit the processes to ensure compliance. Their oversight guarantees that the training pilots receive is rigorous, relevant, and reflective of the industry's highest standards.

The Human Factor: Beyond the Controls

Recurrent training also addresses the human factor, going beyond the controls of the aircraft. It explores topics like crew resource management, fatigue mitigation, and stress management. These sessions equip pilots with the tools to maintain not just aircraft safety but also their personal well-being.

Technology and Training: A Symbiotic Relationship

The symbiotic relationship between technology and training is ever-present. As new systems are introduced into cockpits, training programs evolve to incorporate these advancements. Pilots must become adept at integrating new technologies into their operational repertoire, ensuring they remain at the forefront of the industry.

The Check Airman: Mentor, Evaluator, Guide

The check airman is a mentor, evaluator, and guide. They are the experienced pilots who administer the checks, sharing their wisdom and insights. Their role is to challenge and support, pushing pilots to achieve new heights of capability and confidence.

The Personal Commitment to Excellence

At the heart of recurrent training and checks is the pilot's personal commitment to excellence. It's a dedication that transcends job descriptions and enters the realm of vocation. Pilots who embrace this commitment view training not as a requirement but as an opportunity—a chance to excel, to lead, and to inspire.

Recurrent training and checks are the lifeblood of a pilot's career, the rhythm that sustains their journey through the skies. It's a process that demands dedication, embraces change, and celebrates the pursuit of excellence. For pilots, it's not just about maintaining standards but about exceeding them, about not just flying but soaring.

commanding the skies: the ascent to captaincy

The transition from first officer to captain is a defining moment in the career of a pilot, a rite of passage that marks the culmination of years of dedication, learning, and growth. It's a step that carries with it not just a change in title, but a profound shift in responsibility, authority, and the personal satisfaction of reaching a professional pinnacle.

The Journey Begins

The path to captaincy begins the moment a pilot earns their wings, but the ascent truly gains momentum with each flight hour logged, each challenge met, and each lesson learned. The journey is one of accumulation: hours, experiences, and skills that form the bedrock of a pilot's expertise.

Building Experience

Experience is the currency of aviation, and for a first officer, every flight is an investment in their future. They learn from captains, from situations, and from the very act of flying itself. With each landing, decision, and interaction, they are laying the groundwork for their eventual role as captain.

Leadership in the Making

Leadership is not a switch that is flipped when a pilot

becomes a captain; it is a quality that is nurtured over time. First officers observe their captains, noting how they manage the crew, communicate with passengers, and handle pressure. They take mental notes, often subconsciously, of the traits that make a great leader.

The Crucible of Training

Training is the crucible through which a first officer must pass on their way to captaincy. It's not just about recurrent training or type ratings; it's about specialized leadership courses, advanced decision-making training, and mentorship programs designed to prepare them for command.

The Role of Mentorship

Mentorship plays a vital role in the development of a future captain. Seasoned captains mentor first officers, sharing their wisdom, offering guidance, and providing support. This relationship is invaluable, as it offers a glimpse into the realities of command from those who know it best.

The Assessment of Readiness

The assessment of a first officer's readiness for captaincy is a comprehensive process. It evaluates not just their flying skills, but their ability to lead, to communicate, and to inspire confidence. It's an assessment that looks at the whole person, not just the pilot.

The Weight of Responsibility

With the four stripes of a captain comes a weight of responsibility that is felt from the moment they step into the left seat. Captains are responsible for the safety of the aircraft, the well-being of the passengers, and the performance of the crew. It's a responsibility that is both humbling and exhilarating.

The First Flight as Captain

The first flight as captain is a milestone that is etched in memory. It's a moment of pride, of achievement, and of recognition that the pilot has reached a new level of their profession. It's a flight where training, experience, and instinct converge to create a capable and confident commander.

The Continuous Pursuit of Excellence

Becoming a captain is not the end of the road; it's a new beginning. Captains continue to learn, to grow, and to refine their skills. They stay abreast of changes in the industry, embrace new technologies, and continue to engage in training that challenges and develops them.

The Legacy of Leadership

Captains leave a legacy, not just through the flights they command, but through the first officers they mentor, the crews they lead, and the standards they uphold. They set the tone for what it means to be a pilot, and their influence extends far beyond their own careers.

The ascent to captaincy is a journey that is as challenging as it is rewarding. It's a testament to a pilot's commitment to their craft, their dedication to safety, and their pursuit of excellence. For those who reach this milestone, it's a confirmation that they have not just learned to fly; they have learned to lead.

8 / navigating a pilot's career

charting the course: pilots' pathways in aviation

THE AVIATION INDUSTRY offers a vast horizon of career progression and opportunities for pilots, each path woven with its own set of challenges, learning curves, and rewards. From the first solo flight to the command of a wide-body jet, a pilot's career is a testament to their enduring passion for flight and their commitment to excellence.

The Ascent Begins

For many pilots, the journey begins with small, single-engine aircraft, building hours and experience. But as their logbooks thicken with entries, the skies open up with possibilities. The transition from general aviation to commercial airlines is a significant leap, one that brings pilots into a world of advanced aircraft, diverse routes, and broader responsibilities.

From Regional Routes to International Skies

Many pilots find their first commercial opportunities with regional airlines, where they can gain valuable experience in a multi-crew environment. These positions are often seen as stepping stones, leading to opportunities with larger, international carriers. Each flight, each day, is a step toward a future filled with the promise of crossing continents and oceans.

Specialization: Finding Your Niche

As pilots progress, they may choose to specialize. Some may pursue careers in cargo transport, flying the behemoths of the sky that carry goods across the globe. Others may find their calling in corporate aviation, piloting business jets for companies or private owners. Each specialization offers its own unique set of challenges and rewards, allowing pilots to tailor their careers to their interests and lifestyles.

Instructing: Shaping the Next Generation

For those with a passion for teaching, becoming a flight instructor provides an opportunity to shape the next generation of aviators. Instructors play a crucial role in the industry, passing on their knowledge and experience to students eager to take to the skies. It's a role that demands patience, communication skills, and a deep understanding of aviation pedagogy.

Advancement within the Airline

Within the airline, career progression can take many forms. Some pilots may aspire to become check airmen or training captains, roles that allow them to mentor other pilots and oversee training programs. Others may aim for management positions, where they can influence operations, safety protocols, and the strategic direction of the airline.

The Role of Seniority

Seniority plays a significant role in a pilot's career progression within an airline. It determines everything from the aircraft they fly to their schedules and routes. As pilots climb the seniority ladder, they gain access to more desirable flights and schedules, a reflection of their dedication and time served.

The Pursuit of Higher Education

Some pilots choose to complement their flying careers with higher education. Degrees in aviation management, aerospace engineering, or related fields can open doors to new opportunities both within and outside the cockpit. Education broadens a pilot's perspective, equipping them with the skills to take on leadership roles in the industry.

Advocacy and Industry Involvement

Pilots with a passion for advocacy may become involved in industry organizations, working to shape aviation policy and improve the profession. These roles offer a chance to make a lasting impact on the industry, influencing everything from safety standards to labor relations.

The Entrepreneurial Pilot

Entrepreneurial pilots may venture into business, starting their own aviation-related companies or services. These endeavors require a blend of aviation expertise and business acumen, offering a challenging but potentially rewarding diversion from traditional flying roles.

The Ever-Evolving Industry

The aviation industry is ever-evolving, and with it, the opportunities for pilots continue to expand. Technological advancements, new aircraft, and emerging markets all contribute to a landscape of possibilities for those willing to adapt and grow.

A pilot's career is as dynamic as the skies they navigate. It's a journey marked by continuous learning, adaptation, and a relentless pursuit of new horizons. For those who choose to chart a course in aviation, the opportunities are as boundless as the heavens themselves.

navigating the hierarchy: the influence of seniority in aviation

In the world of aviation, seniority is more than a measure of time—it's a pivotal force that shapes careers, influences daily operations, and impacts the lives of pilots both in and out of the cockpit. This chapter explores the multifaceted impact of seniority, unraveling its complexities and revealing its profound influence on the professional journey of pilots.

The Seniority System: An Established Tradition

The seniority system in aviation is an established tradition, a structured hierarchy that dictates the progression of pilots' careers. It's a ladder that all pilots climb, rung by rung, from the moment they are hired. Seniority determines not just flight assignments and schedules, but also vacation preferences, base assignments, and opportunities for advancement.

The Early Years: Building a Foundation

For new pilots, seniority begins as a constraint. They often fly less desirable routes, work on reserve, and have less control over their schedules. Yet, these early years are a time of growth, where pilots build a foundation of experience and forge relationships that will support them throughout their careers.

The Middle Ranks: Gaining Momentum

As pilots ascend the seniority list, they gain momentum. Their options expand, allowing for more control over their work-life balance. They can bid for preferred routes, enjoy better schedules, and access coveted vacation slots. It's a period of transition, where the benefits of seniority begin to materialize.

The Quest for the Left Seat

Seniority is the key that unlocks the door to the left seat—the captain's chair. The quest for this coveted position is a journey of patience and perseverance. It's a goal that many pilots strive for, and seniority paves the way, marking the passage of time until the opportunity arises.

The Captain's Privilege and Pressure

Once a pilot reaches the rank of captain, seniority offers both privilege and pressure. Captains enjoy the respect that comes with command, but they also bear the weight of responsibility. Their decisions affect not just the safety of the flight, but also the well-being of their crew and passengers.

The Impact on Quality of Life

Seniority has a profound impact on a pilot's quality of life. It influences their daily routines, their time at home, and their ability to attend life's significant events. For many pilots, climbing the seniority list is as much about improving their quality of life as it is about professional advancement.

The Role of Unions and Negotiations

Unions play a critical role in shaping the seniority

system. They negotiate contracts that govern how seniority is applied, ensuring that the system is fair and transparent. These negotiations are a delicate balance of interests, reflecting the needs and desires of pilots at all stages of their careers.

The Challenges of Mergers and Acquisitions

Mergers and acquisitions can disrupt the seniority system, leading to the integration of seniority lists. These events can be times of uncertainty and stress for pilots, as they wait to see how their years of service will be reconciled with those of another airline's pilots.

The Future of Seniority

The future of seniority is a topic of debate. Some argue for reforms that would offer more flexibility, while others defend the system as a cornerstone of the profession. What is certain is that seniority will continue to be a defining element of a pilot's career, shaping their trajectory in ways both seen and unseen.

Embracing the Journey

For pilots, understanding and embracing the seniority system is essential. It's a journey that requires patience, resilience, and a long-term perspective. Seniority is not just about waiting for time to pass; it's about making the most of each moment, each flight, and each opportunity that comes with climbing the ranks.

The impact of seniority in aviation is profound and enduring. It's a system that brings order to the complex world of airline operations, providing a clear path for career progression. For pilots, seniority is a constant companion, a silent force that shapes their careers from the first day on the job to the day they hang up their wings.

broadening horizons: embracing the world stage of aviation

The transition to international flights represents a significant milestone in a pilot's career, marking the expansion of their professional landscape from domestic skies to the vast and varied tapestry of global aviation. It's a shift that brings new challenges, experiences, and the exhilaration of connecting cultures and continents.

The Allure of the International Route

For pilots accustomed to domestic routes, the allure of international flying is often irresistible. It promises the romance of travel, the complexity of cross-border navigation, and the prestige of operating large, long-haul aircraft. It's a realm where the pilot's skills are showcased on the world stage, and their role as an ambassador of the skies comes to the fore.

Preparing for a Global Journey

The preparation for international operations is rigorous. Pilots must familiarize themselves with a broader set of regulations, including international air law, customs protocols, and overflight permissions. They delve into the intricacies of intercontinental weather patterns, oceanic tracks, and the nuances of cross-cultural communication.

Mastering New Aircraft

Often, transitioning to international flights coincides with upgrading to larger aircraft. Pilots undertake extensive training to master the complexities of wide-body jets, which are marvels of modern engineering designed to traverse the globe. The type rating process for these aircraft is a journey of its own, demanding a deep engagement with advanced systems and performance characteristics.

Navigating the Complexities of Time Zones

One of the unique challenges of international flying is managing the impact of multiple time zones. Pilots must adapt to the physiological demands of long-haul travel, mastering the art of managing jet lag and maintaining peak performance despite the body's natural rhythms.

Cultural Competence in the Cockpit

Cultural competence becomes paramount as pilots interact with diverse crews, air traffic controllers, and ground personnel from around the world. They learn the subtleties of language, the importance of cultural sensitivity, and the value of clear, concise communication in a multilingual environment.

Safety and Security on a Global Scale

The safety and security protocols for international flights are heightened. Pilots engage with comprehensive security briefings, become adept at assessing geopolitical risks, and collaborate closely with security agencies to ensure the safety of their flights.

The Rewards of International Operations

The rewards of flying internationally are manifold. Pilots enjoy the satisfaction of commanding some of the most sophisticated aircraft in the world, the pleasure of visiting foreign lands, and the professional pride of operating at the highest levels of their craft.

The Impact on Personal Life

Transitioning to international flights also has a significant impact on a pilot's personal life. The irregular schedules and extended time away from home require a supportive family structure and a resilient personal mindset. Pilots learn to balance their love for flying with the needs of their loved ones, finding harmony in the duality of their lives.

Continued Professional Development

Professional development continues unabated as pilots build their international experience. They attend recurrent training, participate in forums discussing global aviation issues, and often engage in mentorship roles, sharing their knowledge with pilots aspiring to follow in their footsteps.

The Future of International Aviation

As the global aviation landscape evolves, pilots remain at the forefront of change. They adapt to new technologies, changing regulations, and the shifting dynamics of international travel. Their careers are a reflection of the industry's growth and its enduring promise of connecting the world.

Embracing the World Stage

For pilots, transitioning to international flights is about embracing the world stage. It's about expanding their horizons, both literally and figuratively, and playing a pivotal role in the grand ballet of global aviation. It's a chapter in their careers that is written with the contrails of their aircraft, crisscrossing the skies in a testament to their skill, dedication, and the universal human spirit of exploration.

9 / challenges and rewards

harmonizing altitudes: the pilot's quest for work-life balance

IN THE LIFE OF A PILOT, the quest for work-life balance is akin to finding the perfect altitude; it requires constant adjustment, keen awareness, and a commitment to stability amidst the ever-changing conditions of both career and home.

The Unique Rhythms of Aviation

The rhythms of a pilot's life are unique, dictated by flight schedules, time zones, and the demands of safety and precision. These rhythms can be exhilarating, offering a sense of freedom and adventure that few other professions can match. Yet, they also bring challenges to maintaining a harmonious balance between work and personal life.

Crafting a Balanced Flight Plan

Just as a pilot crafts a flight plan with care, so too must they design their life plan. This involves setting clear boundaries, prioritizing time for rest and family, and being proactive in managing the demands of their profession. It's about making intentional choices that align with one's values and goals.

The Turbulence of Time Management

Time management is a critical skill for pilots seeking balance. They must navigate the turbulence of irregular hours, long-haul flights, and layovers. Effective time management means not only maximizing productivity during work hours but also ensuring quality time for relaxation and family.

The Co-Pilot at Home

For many pilots, having a supportive co-pilot at home makes all the difference. Partners who understand the unique pressures of aviation can help maintain equilibrium, sharing responsibilities and providing emotional support during challenging times.

Staying Grounded in Relationships

Staying grounded in relationships is essential for pilots. This means being present during time at home, engaging fully with loved ones, and nurturing relationships that provide a counterweight to the demands of flying.

The Layover Strategy: Maximizing Downtime

Layovers can be seen as opportunities for rest and exploration, but they can also be used strategically to recharge and connect with family through technology. Pilots can use these interludes to maintain relationships, pursue hobbies, or simply rest, ensuring they return to the cockpit refreshed.

The Cumulative Effect of Fatigue

Pilots must be vigilant about the cumulative effect of fatigue. It can erode not only their performance in the cockpit but also their health and well-being. Recognizing the signs of fatigue and taking proactive steps to mitigate it is crucial for maintaining balance.

The Altitude of Perspective

Maintaining perspective is vital. Pilots must remember why they chose to fly and what they cherish about their career. This altitude of perspective helps them weather the inevitable storms and turbulence of a demanding profession.

The Role of the Airline

Airlines also play a role in supporting pilots' work-life balance. Policies that promote flexibility, provide resources for stress management, and recognize the importance of personal time contribute to a more balanced workforce.

Navigating Retirement

Looking toward the horizon, pilots must also navigate the transition to retirement. Planning for this eventual descent from active flying requires foresight and preparation, ensuring that the landing into retirement is as smooth as possible.

Achieving work-life balance as a pilot is an ongoing journey, one that requires self-awareness, support, and the ability to adapt. It's about finding harmony between the passion for flying and the love for life on the ground, ensuring that both are given the attention and care they deserve.

the thrill of flying

Flying is not just a profession or a hobby; it's a calling that beckons to those who look skyward and dream of the freedom that comes with soaring above the clouds. It's a unique blend of art and science, a symphony of aerodynamics, meteorology, and human ambition. For those considering a career as a pilot, the allure of flight is often intertwined with the thrill of mastering complex conversations with air traffic control, navigating through challenging weather, and the satisfaction of a perfectly executed landing.

Engaging with the Skies

Imagine yourself in the cockpit, hands steady on the yoke, eyes scanning the horizon. The radio crackles to life with a symphony of instructions, clearances, and updates. This is where the complexity of pilot conversations begins. Air traffic controllers are your unseen co-pilots, guiding you safely from takeoff to touchdown. Learning their language, understanding their instructions, and responding appropriately is a dance that requires practice, precision, and presence of mind.

Navigating the Unseen Pathways

Airways crisscross the skies like invisible highways. As a pilot, your ability to navigate these pathways hinges on clear communication. You'll learn to interpret aeronautical charts, understand waypoints, and communicate your position with confidence. Each flight is a new opportunity to refine these skills, to become more adept at the intricate dialogue between pilot and sky.

Weathering the Storm

Meteorology is a critical aspect of flying. Pilots must not only understand the science behind the weather but also articulate their needs and intentions when conditions change. Whether it's requesting a route deviation to avoid turbulence or understanding a sudden METAR report, the ability to adapt your conversation to the weather is what makes a competent pilot.

The Harmony of Teamwork

Cockpit resource management is about more than just flying the plane; it's about managing the human elements of flying. It involves clear, concise communication with your co-pilot, crew, and passengers. Each member of the team plays a role in the safety and efficiency of the flight, and as the pilot, you're the conductor of this orchestra.

The Art of the Landing

Landing is often considered the most challenging part of a flight. It's a culmination of all the conversations you've had with air traffic control, your crew, and the aircraft itself. It's about interpreting the feedback from your instruments, feeling the response of the plane, and making split-second decisions. A smooth landing is a testament to the pilot's ability to synthesize information and communicate effectively with the machine.

Continual Growth and Learning

The journey to becoming a pilot is one of continual growth and learning. Each flight builds upon the last, each conversation adds to your repertoire of experience. The thrill of flying comes from the knowledge that with each takeoff, you're not just moving through the air; you're engaging in a complex, dynamic conversation with the world around you.

Flying is more than transportation; it's a conversation with the elements, a negotiation with physics, and a partnership with technology. It's a career that demands the best of your abilities and offers the best of rewards – the sense of freedom, the joy of achievement, and the thrill of taking to the skies. Welcome to the world of aviation, where the sky is not the limit, but the beginning.

financial and personal rewards

Embarking on a career as a pilot is not just about the allure of the skies or the technical mastery of complex machines; it's also about the tangible and intangible rewards that come with this esteemed profession. The financial benefits are often the most immediate to come to mind, but the personal satisfaction and growth that accompany a pilot's life are equally significant.

Economic Altitudes

Let's talk numbers. Pilots are among the highest-paid professionals, with salaries that reflect the skill, expertise, and responsibilities required of the job. Commercial pilots, for instance, can expect a median annual wage that is well above the national average. But it's not just about the paycheck. The financial package for pilots often includes comprehensive health benefits, retirement plans, life insurance, and travel perks that can extend to family members.

Investing in Your Future

Training to become a pilot is an investment in your future. While the initial costs can be substantial, the return on this investment is measured not only in dollars and cents but also in career opportunities. The aviation industry is projected to grow, with increasing demand for commercial pilots due to expanding global travel networks and retiring professionals. This demand translates to job security and the potential for career advancement.

The Currency of Experience

Every hour logged in the cockpit is an investment in your future. With each flight, pilots gain experience that can lead to qualifications for larger aircraft and more complex routes. Seniority brings with it the potential for more desirable routes, schedules, and aircraft types. In the world of aviation, experience is a currency that accrues interest over time, paying dividends in both career progression and personal satisfaction.

A World of Opportunities

The life of a pilot is rich with opportunities for travel and exploration. Pilots see the world from perspectives few others do, visiting destinations across the globe. This exposure to different cultures and places can enrich one's worldview and provide a unique education that extends far beyond the cockpit.

Personal Horizons

Beyond the financial aspects, being a pilot offers a wealth of personal rewards. There's the pride that comes with being part of an elite group of professionals who have mastered the skies. There's the camaraderie among crew members, a bond forged through shared experiences and the collective pursuit of safety and excellence.

Lifelong Learning

Aviation is a field that never stands still, and as a

pilot, you'll be at the forefront of technological and procedural advancements. The pursuit of knowledge is continuous, with recurrent training and certifications keeping your skills sharp and your mind engaged. This commitment to lifelong learning is not just a professional requirement; it's a personal journey that keeps the passion for flying alive.

The Joy of Teaching

For many pilots, the joy of flying is matched by the joy of teaching. Sharing your knowledge with aspiring pilots, whether through formal instruction or mentoring, can be one of the most rewarding aspects of the profession. It's a way to give back to the community that has supported your journey and to help shape the next generation of aviators.

In the end, the life of a pilot is about balance. It's about balancing the technical with the personal, the financial with the experiential. It's about finding harmony between the demands of the job and the rewards it offers. For those who hear the call of the skies, the journey is as rewarding as the destination. The career of a pilot is a path paved with challenges, but each one is an opportunity to ascend to new heights, personally and professionally. Welcome aboard the journey of a lifetime.

10 / the future of aviation

technological advancements: elevating aviation conversations

THE COCKPIT of an aircraft is a hub of technological marvels, a testament to human ingenuity and the relentless pursuit of safety and efficiency in aviation. As a pilot, you'll find yourself at the intersection of time-honored flying principles and cutting-edge advancements that transform how you interact with your aircraft and the world around you.

The Digital Revolution in the Skies

Gone are the days of bulky flight manuals and cumbersome maps. The digital age has ushered in an era of sleek glass cockpits, where touchscreens and Head-Up Displays (HUDs) provide critical information at a glance.

These advancements not only streamline the pilot's workflow but also enhance the complexity and depth of conversations between pilots and their machines.

Autopilot: A Trusted Co-Pilot

The autopilot system is a marvel that has evolved significantly over the years. Today's systems are capable of handling a multitude of tasks, from maintaining altitude to complex navigational procedures. Learning to communicate effectively with this automated co-pilot—inputting precise commands and understanding its feedback—is a skill that epitomizes the modern pilot's repertoire.

Connectivity at Altitude

In-flight connectivity has revolutionized how pilots communicate with the ground and each other. Real-time weather updates, live traffic information, and instant messaging with air traffic control are now at your fingertips, enabling more informed and dynamic decision-making in the air.

Simulation: The Virtual Skies

Flight simulators have become incredibly sophisticated, providing a virtual environment that replicates the flying experience with remarkable accuracy. These simulators allow pilots to engage in complex scenarios, honing their communication skills with air traffic control and crew without leaving the ground.

Unmanned Aerial Systems: The New Frontier

Drones and unmanned aerial vehicles (UAVs) are the new players in the airspace, and they bring a whole new dimension to aviation conversations. Pilots must now be versed in the language and regulations of UAV operations, ensuring safe and harmonious integration into the airspace.

Data Analysis: Beyond the Flight

Post-flight data analysis tools offer a wealth of information that can be used to debrief and improve future flights. By examining this data, pilots can engage in more nuanced conversations about performance, safety, and efficiency, both with themselves and with their peers.

The Human Element: CRM Evolved

Crew Resource Management (CRM) has always been about effective communication. With technological advancements, CRM now encompasses a broader range of tools and systems that facilitate better teamwork and decision-making in the cockpit.

Safety Systems: Conversations for Survival

Emergency and safety systems in modern aircraft are designed to communicate critical information quickly and clearly. Understanding these alerts and responding appropriately is a conversation that can mean the difference between safety and disaster.

As technology continues to advance, so too does the

complexity and sophistication of conversations in aviation. From digital cockpits to UAVs, each technological leap requires pilots to adapt, learn, and communicate in new and more complex ways. Embracing these advancements is key to not just becoming a pilot, but excelling as one. The future of aviation is bright, and it speaks in a language of innovation and progress—a language that you, as a pilot, will come to know and speak fluently. Welcome to the cutting edge of aviation, where every conversation takes you higher.

the role of pilots in future aviation

As we gaze into the future of aviation, it's clear that pilots will continue to play a pivotal role in the ever-evolving tapestry of air travel and exploration. With technological advancements surging forward, the pilot's role is transforming, requiring a new level of adaptability and a deeper understanding of complex systems and conversations.

Pilots as Technological Conduits

The pilots of tomorrow are not just operators of machines; they are interpreters and conduits of advanced technology. They must possess the ability to seamlessly integrate sophisticated systems into the flying experience, ensuring that human expertise and machine intelligence work in concert to achieve new heights of safety and efficiency.

Masters of Multidimensional Communication

The complexity of pilot conversations will expand beyond the traditional two-dimensional exchanges with air traffic control and crew. Pilots will engage with AI co-pilots, ground operators, and even passengers in a more interactive and multidimensional manner. This will require a mastery of new communication tools and protocols, as well as an ability to make real-time decisions based on a deluge of data.

Safety and Security Ambassadors

As the guardians of the skies, pilots must be at the forefront of advocating for and implementing enhanced safety and security measures. Their role will involve not only adhering to these protocols but also shaping them through proactive communication with regulatory bodies and industry leaders.

Environmental Stewards

The future of aviation is inextricably linked to environmental stewardship. Pilots will need to engage in conversations about sustainable practices, fuel efficiency, and emissions reduction. They will become key players in the industry's efforts to combat climate change, requiring a thorough understanding of environmental impacts and mitigation strategies.

Educators and Mentors

Experienced pilots will find themselves in the role of

educators, passing on their knowledge to a new generation of aviators. They will be responsible for crafting the complex conversations that inspire and instruct, ensuring that the legacy of flight continues to thrive in an era of rapid change.

Innovators and Visionaries

The pilot's seat is also a vantage point for innovation. Pilots will contribute to the development of new aircraft designs, navigation systems, and operational procedures. Their insights, born from countless hours at the controls, will be invaluable in shaping the future of aviation.

The role of pilots in future aviation is not just about flying; it's about leading the charge into a new era. It's about being the human element that connects the past, present, and future of flight. As technology advances, the pilot's role will become more complex, but also more critical. They will be the ones who ensure that as the industry grows and changes, the essence of aviation—the thrill of flight, the commitment to safety, and the joy of discovery—remains strong. Welcome to the cockpit of the future, where every flight is a step into the unknown, and every pilot is a pioneer.

preparing for changes in the industry

The aviation industry is a dynamic and ever-evolving field, shaped by technological advancements, economic shifts, and global trends. As a pilot, preparing for these changes is not just about staying current with certifications and training; it's about embracing a mindset of flexibility and continuous improvement. It's about being ready to engage in complex conversations that will shape your career and the future of aviation.

Adapting to Technological Shifts

The cockpit of the future will continue to evolve, with new instruments, systems, and automation becoming standard. Staying abreast of these changes means pilots must be lifelong learners, always ready to master new technologies. It's about understanding the implications of these tools on your role and being able to articulate these changes to colleagues and stakeholders.

Understanding Economic Winds

Economic fluctuations can have a significant impact on the aviation industry. From fuel prices to airline mergers, pilots must be conversant in the language of economics to navigate their careers successfully. This involves not just understanding the factors that affect the industry but also being able to discuss them in the broader context of global economics.

Navigating Regulatory Airspace

Regulations are the framework within which the aviation industry operates. As these regulations change in response to new technologies and societal demands, pilots must be prepared to engage in the conversation.

This means staying informed about proposed changes, understanding their impact, and even participating in the dialogue that shapes these regulations.

Cultivating Professional Relationships

Networking within the industry is more important than ever. Building relationships with other professionals can provide insights into changes on the horizon and help you prepare for them. These connections are also vital for career advancement and finding new opportunities as the industry evolves.

Embracing Environmental Responsibility

Environmental concerns are becoming increasingly central to the aviation conversation. Pilots must be prepared to discuss and implement strategies for reducing the environmental impact of flying. This includes understanding carbon offsetting, fuel efficiency, and the role of alternative fuels in future aviation.

Anticipating Passenger Expectations

Passenger expectations are changing, with a greater emphasis on personalized experiences and digital services. Pilots will need to be part of the conversation about how to meet these expectations while maintaining the highest safety standards.

Preparing for changes in the aviation industry requires a proactive approach to learning and communication. It's about being informed, adaptable, and ready to engage in the complex conversations that will define the future of flying. As a pilot, you are not just a passenger on this journey; you are a navigator, helping to steer the course of an entire industry. Welcome to a world where change is the only constant, and your ability to adapt is your greatest asset.

epilogue: beyond the horizon

continuing education and growth

The journey of a pilot is one of perpetual ascent, where the horizon of knowledge expands with every flight. In the world of aviation, the commitment to continuing education and growth is not merely a professional requirement; it's a personal ethos that defines the most successful and fulfilled pilots. This chapter delves into the essence of lifelong learning in the cockpit and beyond, exploring how pilots can cultivate a mindset geared toward continuous improvement and deeper engagement with the multifaceted conversations of their craft.

The Lifelong Learner's Flight Plan

Education for pilots doesn't end with the acquisition of a license; it's an ongoing process that spans an entire career. The aviation industry is characterized by rapid technological advancements, regulatory updates, and evolving best practices. Staying at the forefront of these changes requires a proactive approach to learning. Pilots must regularly engage with new materials, attend workshops, and participate in recurrent training sessions. This dedication ensures that they remain not just competent, but proficient and ahead of the curve.

Advanced Ratings and Certifications

One of the most straightforward paths to growth is through the pursuit of additional ratings and certifications. Whether it's an instrument rating, a multi-engine license, or a type rating for a specific aircraft, each new qualification enhances a pilot's skill set and opens up new avenues for professional development. These certifications are more than just accolades; they represent a pilot's commitment to mastering the complexities of their profession.

Mentorship and Peer Learning

The cockpit is a classroom, and every flight is a lesson. Experienced pilots have a wealth of knowledge to share, and mentorship is a powerful tool for growth. Engaging in conversations with seasoned aviators provides invaluable insights that can't be found in textbooks. Similarly, peer learning among colleagues offers a platform for pilots to exchange experiences, discuss challenges, and collectively enhance their understanding of the art of flying.

Academic Pursuits

For those who wish to delve deeper into the theoretical underpinnings of aviation, academic programs offer a structured approach to learning. Degrees in aeronautical science, aviation management, or aerospace engineering can provide pilots with a broader perspective on the industry. These programs foster critical thinking and complex problem-solving skills, equipping pilots to engage in higher-level conversations about the future of aviation.

Simulator Training: The Virtual Skies

Simulation technology has become a cornerstone of pilot training, offering a risk-free environment to practice emergency procedures, perfect instrument approaches, and refine decision-making skills. Advanced simulators can replicate nearly any scenario, allowing pilots to prepare for the unexpected and make more informed choices in the real world. The lessons learned in the simulator are directly transferable to the cockpit, enhancing a pilot's ability to navigate complex situations.

Industry Engagement

Active participation in aviation organizations and industry events is another avenue for growth. These platforms provide opportunities to stay updated on the latest developments, network with professionals, and contribute to the discourse shaping the future of flying. By engaging with the industry at large, pilots can influence change and ensure their voice is heard in the ongoing conversation about aviation's trajectory.

Personal Development

Continuing education is not limited to aviation-specific knowledge. Personal development, including skills such as leadership, communication, and stress management, plays a crucial role in a pilot's growth. These skills enhance a pilot's ability to lead a crew, interact with passengers, and manage the demands of the job. They also contribute to a pilot's ability to make complex conversations more effective, whether in the cockpit or in life.

Embracing Technology

In an era where technology is reshaping the landscape of aviation, pilots must be adept at integrating new tools into their practice. From electronic flight bags (EFBs) to data analytics platforms, the modern pilot must be conversant with digital innovations. Understanding how to leverage these technologies for planning, navigation, and communication is essential for staying relevant and effective in the profession.

Epilogue: Beyond the Horizon

retirement and legacy

The flight path of a pilot's career is long and filled with countless takeoffs and landings, each marking a significant moment in a lifelong journey of growth, challenges, and achievements. As pilots navigate through their careers, the time eventually comes to consider retirement and the legacy they will leave behind. This chapter explores the transition into retirement, the importance of planning for this phase, and how pilots can continue to contribute to the aviation community, shaping the conversations and the future of flying even after they have left the cockpit.

Charting the Course to Retirement

Retirement planning is an essential conversation that pilots must have with themselves, their families, and financial advisors. It's about more than just ensuring financial security; it's about envisioning a future that continues to be rich in purpose and fulfillment. Pilots are encouraged to think about retirement early in their careers, setting goals and investing wisely to ensure a smooth transition from active flying to a new chapter of life.

The Final Approach

As pilots near retirement, they often reflect on their careers, considering the flights they've piloted and the impact they've had on others. It's a time to pass on wisdom, to mentor younger pilots, and to ensure that the values and lessons learned in the air are not lost. This transfer of knowledge is crucial, as it helps to maintain the high standards of the profession and prepares the next generation to take the controls.

A Legacy of Safety and Excellence

Pilots leave a legacy through their commitment to safety and excellence. Throughout their careers, they contribute to the collective knowledge of the aviation community, participating in safety programs, sharing experiences, and sometimes helping to develop new protocols and procedures. In retirement, they have the opportunity to continue this work, perhaps through consulting, writing, or speaking engagements, further solidifying their contributions to the field.

Continued Engagement with Aviation

Retirement doesn't mean the end of a pilot's relationship with aviation. Many retired pilots find new ways to stay connected to the community they love. Some may choose to fly recreationally, while others might volunteer with aviation nonprofits, serve on advisory boards, or even take up flight instructing to share their passion and expertise with new pilots.

The Pilot's Role in Shaping the Future

Even in retirement, pilots have a role in shaping the future of aviation. Their insights and experiences are invaluable in complex conversations about the direction of the industry. They can advocate for advancements in technology, improvements in training, and the overall betterment of aviation. Their voices are respected and needed in the ongoing dialogue about how to make flying safer, more efficient, and more accessible.

Embracing New Horizons

Retirement is also a time for pilots to explore new horizons and pursue interests that may have been set aside during their busy flying careers. Whether it's traveling, taking up new hobbies, or spending more time with family and friends, retirement offers a wealth of opportunities to enjoy the fruits of a career well-flown.

The retirement of a pilot is not an end but a new beginning. It's a time to reflect on a career spent among the clouds, to take pride in the accomplishments and the journey, and to look forward to the future with anticipation and excitement. The conversations that pilots have throughout their careers—about safety, technology, and the joy of flying—don't end with retirement. Instead, they take on new dimensions, continuing to influence and inspire long after the last flight has been logged. Welcome to the next chapter, where the legacy of a pilot becomes a guiding light for those who continue to reach for the sky.

Epilogue: Beyond the Horizon

inspiring the next generation of pilots

The baton of aviation is passed from one generation to the next, not just through logbooks and licenses, but through stories, experiences, and the shared passion for flight. As we consider the future of aviation, it becomes imperative to inspire and nurture the next wave of pilots —those who will push the boundaries of what's possible in the skies and continue the legacy of those who came before them.

The Power of Mentorship

Mentorship is the cornerstone of pilot development. It's the process through which wisdom is imparted, skills are honed, and the flame of passion for flying is kindled in the hearts of aspiring aviators. Experienced pilots have a treasure trove of knowledge that, when shared, can light the way for newcomers to navigate the complexities of the aviation world.

Sharing the Journey

Every pilot's journey is a story, and these narratives are the threads that weave the rich tapestry of aviation history. By sharing the highs and lows, the triumphs and tribulations, seasoned pilots can offer a realistic yet inspiring picture of what it means to pursue a career in the skies. These stories serve as powerful tools for engaging in meaningful conversations with those considering the pilot's path.

Fostering a Community of Learning

Aviation thrives on community—a fellowship of individuals united by their love for flight. Encouraging the next generation to participate in this community, whether through aviation clubs, online forums, or industry events, is vital. It's in these communal spaces that aspiring pilots can engage in dialogue, ask questions, and build the relationships that will support them throughout their careers.

Emphasizing the Importance of Education

The role of education in shaping a pilot's career cannot be overstated. It's not just about the technical knowledge required to operate an aircraft; it's about understanding the broader context of aviation, including its history, its impact on society, and its potential for the future. Encouraging ongoing education and a thirst for knowledge is essential for the development of well-rounded, competent pilots.

Advocating for Diversity and Inclusion

The future of aviation depends on a diverse and inclusive cohort of pilots. By advocating for and supporting initiatives that promote diversity in the cockpit, the current generation of pilots can help ensure that the next generation reflects the rich variety of backgrounds and perspectives that make up our world. This diversity enriches the conversations within the industry and leads to more innovative and effective solutions to the challenges faced by aviators.

Utilizing Technology as a Teaching Tool

Technology has transformed the way we learn and communicate. For the next generation of pilots, simulators, virtual reality, and online training platforms will be integral to their education. Current pilots can leverage these tools to create engaging and interactive learning experiences that resonate with tech-savvy newcomers.

Encouraging Professional Development

The path to becoming a pilot is marked by continuous professional development. By encouraging aspiring pilots to seek out additional certifications, attend workshops, and pursue leadership opportunities, experienced aviators can help them build the skills necessary for a successful career in aviation.

Leading by Example

Perhaps the most powerful way to inspire the next generation is to lead by example. Pilots who demonstrate professionalism, integrity, and a commitment to excellence in their own careers serve as living proof of the rewards that come with a life in aviation. They show that, while the journey may be demanding, the view from the cockpit is worth every challenge faced along the way.

Inspiring the next generation of pilots is a responsibility that falls on the shoulders of all who have been

Epilogue: Beyond the Horizon

captivated by the call of the skies. It's about passing on not just knowledge and skills, but a sense of wonder and possibility. It's about engaging in conversations that spark curiosity, foster ambition, and encourage perseverance. As we look to the future, we do so with the confidence that the next generation of pilots will carry the legacy of flight to new horizons, propelled by the inspiration and guidance of those who came before them. Welcome to the vanguard of aviation, where every word spoken, every lesson taught, and every story shared helps to launch the dreams of those who will write the next chapter in the story of flight.